Glass

GLASS

FROM CINDERELLA'S SLIPPERS
TO FIBER OPTICS

RUTH G. KASSINGER

Material World

Twenty-First Century Books
Brookfield, Connecticut

To Betty Good Edelson

Cover photograph courtesy of Photri-Microstock
Photographs courtesy of SuperStock: pp. 4 (Hermitage Museum, St. Petersburg, Russia/Leonid Bogdanov), 32, 67; The Corning Museum of Glass: pp. 6, 20, 38, 40, 47 (bottom); Erich Lessing/Art Resource, NY: pp. 8, 10, 17; Chihuly Hotshop/Seattle, Washington: p. 12 (Theresa Batty), 13 (Theresa Batty), 64 (© Scott M. Lee), 65 (© Russell Johnson); Art Resource, NY: p. 14; Peter Arnold, Inc.: pp. 18 (© James L. Amos), 56 (© James L. Amos); © George Payne www.cajunimages.com: p. 26; Photo Researchers, Inc.: pp. 27 (© Richard Hutchings), 66 (top left © Tim Davis; bottom left © Alain Dex/Publiphoto; right © Joseph Nettis); © Tom Pantages: pp. 28 (both); The British Museum: p. 41; Scala/Art Resource, NY: p. 43; Photri-Microstock: pp. 47 (top), 54; Victoria & Albert Museum, London/Art Resource: p. 49; Réunion des Musées Nationaux/Art Resource, NY: p. 52; Corbis: p. 58 (© David Samuel Robbins.. Map by Joe LeMonnier.

Library of Congress Cataloging-in-Publication Data
Kassinger, Ruth, 1954-
Glass : from Cinderella's slippers to fiber optics / Ruth G. Kassinger.
p. cm. -- (Material world)
Summary: Describes the physical composition and characteristics of glass, and presents glassmaking techniques and the various uses made of glass throughout history.
Includes bibliographical references and index.
ISBN 0-7613-2109-8
1. Glass--Juvenile literature. [1. Glass.] I. Title.
TP857.3 .K37 2003   620.1'44--dc21   2002005329

Published by Twenty-First Century Books
A Division of The Millbrook Press, Inc.
2 Old New Milford Road
Brookfield, Connecticut 06804
www.millbrookpress.com

Venetian glass object from the nineteenth century

Contents

This star pendant made 1450–1350 B.C. is one of the earliest pieces of Mesopotamian glass to have been found.

CHAPTER ONE

The Beginning of Glass

THE FIRST GLASS

A long time ago, so the ancient story goes, sailors pulled their boats up on the sandy shores of a river that flowed into the Mediterranean Sea in what is today Syria. The sailors were Phoenicians, great traders around 1000 B.C., and they set up camp and prepared to cook their dinner. They had a problem, however. There were no large rocks or timbers to support their cooking pot. So they unloaded a few blocks of natron, a valuable mineral used in preserving mummies, from their cargo and built a hot fire between the blocks on the sand. After the fire had blazed for a while, the sailors were surprised to see that some of the natron vanished and some liquid was running out from the fire. When the liquid cooled, they discovered that it was a new material, glass.

It's a good story, but it isn't true. In fact, the first man-made glass was created about 2500 B.C. by the Mesopotamians, a people who lived in what is now Iraq, long before the Phoenicians existed as a people. Mesopotamian glassmakers fashioned opaque (not clear) glass beads in a variety of colors and other small pieces of jewelry.

SECRETS OF GLASSMAKING

For a thousand years glass was a curiosity. It was not until about 1500 B.C. in Egypt that glassmaking became an art and industry. The Egyptians may have learned about glassmaking when warriors under Pharaoh Thutmose III conquered Mesopotamia. Or perhaps they discovered the secrets of glassmaking independently. In any case, the Egyptians were well stocked with the major ingredients of glass—silica, sodium carbonate, and calcium oxide—in addition to having skilled craftsmen who could turn those ingredients into glass.

The most important glassmaking ingredient, silica, is a compound of silicon, a chemical element that makes up about one-quarter of the Earth's crust. We see silica most often as sand. The best sand for glassmaking is not

The intense heat of volcanoes melts quartz deep in the Earth into a kind of glass called *obsidian*. Obsidian is usually black, and when it is chipped, it has remarkably sharp edges. Early humans shaped pieces of obsidian to make cutting tools. When the Spaniards attacked the Aztecs in Mexico in the sixteenth century, they found that the Aztecs' obsidian knives were sharper than their steel swords.

beach sand. Although beach sand is mainly silica, it also has lots of shell fragments and other minerals and metals. The sand that is best is the kind that is full of crystals that glitter in the sun and can be found in many parts of the world. Those glittery crystals are quartz, which is another name for silica.

With today's furnaces, glassmakers can achieve the temperature of about 3100°F (1700°C) that it takes to make a pure silica glass. But the ancient glassmakers couldn't come close to that temperature. Fortunately, glassmakers discovered that if they added sodium carbonate (also called soda or soda ash) to the sand, it lowered the melting temperature of the sand. They found sodium carbonate as a natural mineral deposit and as a substance in the burned remains of plants. The Egyptians used natron, a mineral that contains sodium carbonate.

One other ingredient essential for making ancient glass was calcium oxide, also called lime, a mineral found in limestone, chalk, and seashells. Lime prevents glass from dissolving in water.

It takes high heat to combine these ingredients to make glass. Egyptian glassmakers put the silica, natron, and lime into a fired (heat-hardened) clay pot and put the pot into a hot kiln. After about twenty-four hours, the glass ingredients reached about 1500°F (800°C) and melted into a glowing, red-hot, thick liquid called a *melt*. The hotter the temperature of the melt, the more liquid it became.

The Egyptians were probably the first people to make glass bottles. First, the bottle maker would form a "core" of clay and sand mixed with dung around the end of an iron rod. He fash-

This 4-inch (10-cm) bottle, made in Egypt about 1400 B.C. with the core method, held oils that noblewomen used as cosmetics and perfumes. In ancient Egypt, only the very wealthy could afford glass.

ioned the core in the shape of the bottle he planned to make. Then he dipped the rod with the core into the melt, rotated it, and pulled it out. As the glass began to cool a little, he rolled the glass-covered core on a flat stone to make a smooth surface. He repeated the process several times, adding layers of molten glass until the glass was sturdy.

After the bottle cooled, the bottle maker might decorate it. To do so, he would dip another rod into a pot of brightly colored molten glass and trail threads of glass around the outside of the bottle. While the decoration was still hot and soft, he ran a comb through the threads to make a wavy pattern. When the bottle was cool, the glassmaker scratched out the core of sand and clay from the inside.

ROMAN GLASS

Molten glass has the consistency of thick honey. It can be poured into a mold or rolled (but not with bare hands!) into a rod. If you dip a metal rod in a pot of molten glass and then pull it out slowly, you can pull out a long string of glass. Pull the rod out more quickly while turning it, and you can get a glowing glob (called a *gather*) of glass on the end. If you have a hollow iron rod (a *blowpipe*) and you blow gently into the gather on the end, the gather will form a bubble of glass.

The ancient Mesopotamians were probably the first to discover that glass could be blown, but it was the Romans who made glassblowing an industry about A.D. 100. Roman glassblowers perfected techniques for glassblowing and turned out thousands of drinking glasses and other glass containers. Ordinary people—not just the wealthy—were able to afford glass drinking cups, bowls, and containers. The ancient Romans (like people today) liked drinking out of glass containers because their eyes, as well as their taste buds, could take pleasure in what they were drinking.

The Art of Glassblowing

Machines produce almost all of our glassware today, but glassblowers, such as these from the Chihuly workshop in Seattle, Washington, still make special glass objects using ancient glassmaking techniques.

To begin the glassblowing process, the glassblower dips his blowpipe into the furnace to get a gather of molten red-hot glass. The glassblower then lets the excess drip off like honey from a spoon.

Next, using a blowpipe, the glassblower enlarges the piece by blowing through the tube to create a glass bubble. The blower makes sure he never breathes in through the blowpipe because the heat would burn his lungs.

The glassblower also shapes the object by rolling it on a steel table to smooth its sides. This process is called *marvering*.

Glassblowing is a team effort. Controlling the form of the glass requires constant spinning, shaping, and reheating. Here, glassblowers use a paddle to shape the elongated bubble of glass.

When the piece reaches a desired shape, the glassblower attaches a *pontil* rod to the other end of the still fiery hot cylinder and detaches it from the blowpipe. Then the glassblower can reheat the object, shape the end where the blowpipe was attached, and finish the cylinder.

After the piece is complete, it will be placed in an *annealing* (cooling) *oven*, which allows it to cool slowly over a period of twenty-four to seventy-two hours. Glass must be annealed slowly or it will break.

The Roman glassblowers invented and often used *mold-blowing* to make identical bottles, glasses, dishes, and other containers. First, the glassblower blew a red-hot bubble of glass about the size of the object he wished to make. A helper stood by with an iron mold, which was made of two hinged halves. (One popular mold made a flask in the shape of a bunch of grapes.) When the glassblower decided that the glass was just the right temperature, based on the shade of red of the hot glass, the helper closed the mold around the glass bubble. The glassblower continued to blow into the blowpipe in order to force glass into all parts of the mold. After a few moments, the mold was opened again and out came a transparent but still extremely hot glass bottle or vase.

Roman glassmakers also invented *cameo glass*. Cameo glass was made with layers of dark glass, which were then overlaid with layers of white glass. An artist cut away much of the white glass so that a dark background was left. The glassworker then sculpted the remaining, slightly raised, white glass into a scene, often an incident from a myth.

ISLAMIC GLASS

With the fall of the Roman Empire in the late fifth century, glassmaking in Europe fell into a decline. Glassmaking flourished, though, in the Middle East starting in the seventh century. There, artists used brilliantly colored *enamel* (glass-based) paints and gold to decorate the exterior surfaces of blown-glass containers and goblets. They also learned how to paint a film of oil mixed with silver, copper, or gold on a glass object. Once

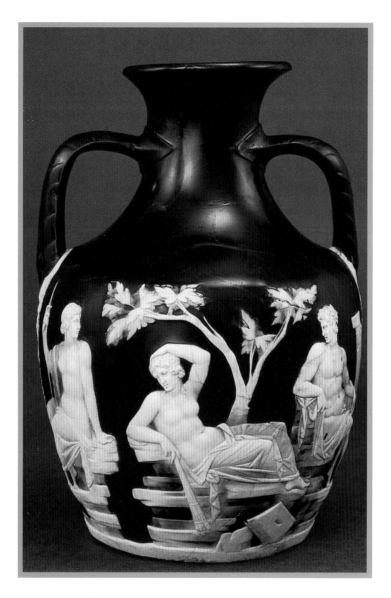

The Portland Vase, now in
the British Museum, is the most famous example
of Roman cameo glass.

heated, the metallic oil became a part of the glass and turned it a glittering amber color. The technique is called *luster painting*.

The center of Middle Eastern glassmaking was Damascus, a city in modern Syria. But Damascus was invaded by Tamerlane, a violent and cruel warlord from Uzbekistan (in Central Asia) who conquered much of the Middle East in the late 1300s. After devastating the city, Tamerlane carried off the glassmakers to Samarkand, his capital in Uzbekistan, and the greatest era of Islamic glass came to an end.

STAINED GLASS

European glassware in the medieval era, roughly 700 to 1300, was simple and unsophisticated. The few fine goblets, vases, plates, and bowls used by Europeans in this period were imported from the Middle East. Medieval Europeans did, however, advance glassmaking technology in a new direction in one important area: stained glass window making.

The Romans had pioneered the *cylinder glass method* of making flat glass for windows, and the glassmakers in Gaul (part of modern France) carried on the tradition. To make a piece of flat glass, a glassblower of the time first blew a gather into a sphere and then, by rolling the still-hot sphere on a piece of stone or metal, shaped it into a cylinder. He then cut the cylinder down its length with a pair of scissors. After reheating the cut cylinder to soften it, he flattened it into a sheet and let it cool.

A medieval window maker could also make a small piece of flat glass in another way. After blowing a large bubble of glass, he attached a pontil to the other side of the hot bubble and broke off the blowpipe. He then twirled the pontil so that cen-

The stained glass windows of Chartres,
a medival cathedral near Paris, are world renowned.
Note the rich colors and exquisite design.

trifugal force caused the bubble to spread out into a *crown*, a round piece of glass. Crown glass tended to be thinner around the edges and thick in the center where the pontil had been attached. The differing thicknesses of crown glass distorted light, and for this reason, crown glass was not used for the highest quality stained glass windows.

Glassmakers colored glass by adding metal compounds to the melt. They discovered that tin produces white glass, copper produces greens and blues, cobalt makes blues, manganese makes purples and browns, gold makes ruby red, and silver produces yellow. Expert glassmakers could produce a rainbow of colors by careful additions to the melting pot.

Stained glass window artists also painted directly on the glass. They used a dark brown enamel paint called *grisaille*. Then, by heating a painted window in an oven, they permanently fused the paint to the glass. Sometimes they painted over a large section of glass and then scratched off the paint to make the design or picture.

Before the glassblower made the first piece of glass, he or an artist created the design for the window. Early medieval stained glass artists drew their designs, indicating the size and color of all the individual pieces of glass, on a large table that had been painted white. After the glassblower made pieces of glass, a glass cutter cut the pieces to the shapes indicated on the table. The artist painted those pieces that required painting and heated them in the oven to fix the paint. He then put the pieces together like pieces of a jigsaw puzzle by sinking their edges into thin strips of lead, called *cames*. Finally, the artist outlined the entire panel with cames and installed it in the window opening.

About the year 1000, stained glass found its place in northern European churches. At this time, the economy of Europe was recovering from centuries of barbarian invasions, harsh weather, and deaths from the plague. Gradually, farmers began to use better techniques and tools to grow more crops. Artisans became more skilled and productive. Towns grew in population and wealth. Because this was an age of great religious belief, people began to contribute some of their new wealth to the building of churches. Towns vied with one another to build the most beautiful churches. The richly colored stained glass windows that seemed to pour the glory of God down on the congregants also reflected the pride of the citizens who paid for their creation. For the next three centuries, glass artists painted in glass, color, and light, making people's spirits soar.

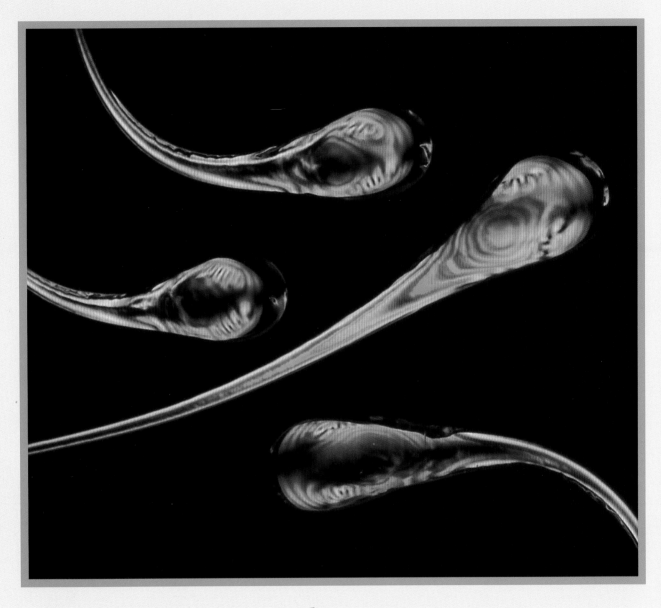

These are modern Prince Rupert's Drops.

CHAPTER TWO

Magical Glass

One day, sometime in the 1640s, Prince Rupert of Bavaria arrived in England to visit his English grandfather, King James I. He arrived with a present of several small teardrops of glass, which he placed on the table before the king and his attendants. They were lovely, delicate objects that tapered gracefully into long, curved, and exquisitely thin tails. Prince Rupert then took out a hammer and slammed it down on the head of one of the teardrops. To everyone's amazement, the glass drop was unharmed. Next, Prince Rupert picked up the glass teardrop, put it in his palm, and pinched off the very end of the tail. Instantly, the glass drop exploded! All that remained in the prince's palm was a small mound of white glass dust.

The glass drops, which became known as *Prince Rupert's Drops,* seemed utterly magical. In the seventeenth century, no one understood why a glass drop that could withstand a direct hammer blow would explode into dust when a tiny piece of its tail was broken. (You'll find out why in Chapter Three.) But the mystery just seemed to be one more example of the magical nature of glass.

Even the process of making glass seemed magical. First, there was the mystery of how three common, opaque materials—sand, ashes, and lime—could combine into such an extraordinary substance as clear glass. Then there was the awe-inspiring setting for glassmaking. The glassmaker kept part of his workshop dark because he needed to see the color of the molten glass to judge when it was ready to be blown or shaped. His furnace radiated tremendous heat and when he opened the small door to it, he seemed to have opened a fiery eye. With the glassblower's breath, the glass gather on the end of a blowpipe appeared to come alive, growing, swelling, and changing shape like some fantastical spirit. If ever there was a home for magic, it was in the glassmaker's workshop!

Finally, there were the qualities of glass itself. It could be clear as air, yet solid as stone. Glass could be pulled into a delicate thread that trembled in a breeze, yet an edge of glass could cut like a knife. Terribly fragile when blown into a goblet, when formed into a brick it could support the weight of an elephant. In a prism shape, it split sunlight into a rainbow of colors. In a sphere, it distorted the world into grotesque shapes. In a mirror, it reflected whatever appeared before it.

One modern scientist, George Kunz, has a theory for why so many people believed they could read the future in a crystal ball. He thinks the points of reflected light from the highly polished surface of a rock crystal or glass ball tire the optic nerve in the viewer's eye. Then, says Kunz, the nerve stops transmitting images from the outside and instead sends images from inside the brain.

GLASS MAGIC

Rock crystal is clear natural quartz formed entirely from silica molecules joined together at great pressure deep in the earth. In the ancient world, magicians gazed into a highly polished sphere of rock crystal and proclaimed that they could see the future in its depths. By the fifth century in Europe, scrying (crystal ball gazing) became very popular. In the Middle Ages, the Church condemned crystal ball gazing as a pagan practice, but the practice didn't die out. The crystal clarity of the balls was simply too entrancing.

Even though most people today no longer believe crystal balls can tell the future, their magic lives on in our imaginations. In the movie version of *The Wizard of Oz*, after Dorothy is captured by the Wicked Witch of the West, she spots a crystal ball in the room where she is imprisoned. As she looks into the ball, she magically sees her Auntie Em back in Kansas, worrying about her. You can still find people who claim to see the future in a crystal ball . . . and people who believe them.

Glass balls held other kinds of magic. Irish sailors' wives once hung blown glass balls in their windows to assure their husbands' safe return. Eastern Europeans hung them from their ceilings as protection against evil spirits. In late-seventeenth-century England, people hung similar objects, called *witches' balls*, in their windows, porches, or inside the front door in order to prevent evil spirits and mischievous fairies from entering.

Witches' balls were filled with holy water or special herbs. Later, people came to appreciate the balls for their beauty alone, and factories made them in colors and with delicate threads of glass looping through their interiors. You can find stores that sell witches' balls today.

The mystery of glass has played a part in many fairy tales. Most famous are the glass slippers that Cinderella wears in Frenchman Charles Perrault's seventeenth-century fairy tale. Without Cinderella's lost glass slipper, the prince would never have found her. In several tales from Europe, evil characters whisk away princesses to the top of glass mountains. Only the bravest, cleverest heroes are able to scale the glass. In a Hungarian tale, "The Glass Axe," the hero is trapped by an evil fairy who commands him to chop down an entire forest with a glass axe or face a horrible punishment. This seems, of course, to be an impossible task, but glass is a mysterious material and it turns out that his axe is up to the job.

MIRROR MAGIC

When the Venetians learned to put a backing of silver on a sheet of glass to make a mirror, mirrors also became magical. In the nineteenth-century fairy tale by the Brothers Grimm, the evil stepmother asks her magic mirror, "Magic mirror on the wall: Who's the fairest of us all?" The magical mirror speaks (truthfully, of course, because mirrors reflect reality) and replies that Snow White is the most beautiful one in the kingdom.

People believed that mirrors, like crystal balls, could predict the future. John Dee, court magician to Queen Elizabeth I, used one. It was said that he used a magic mirror to foretell the plot to kill King James in 1605. Because mirrors were thought to hold the key to the future, to break one was to shatter your own future. It is a superstition in many cultures that breaking a mirror will bring you a certain period of bad luck. But as long as you didn't break them, mirrors were believed to ward off evil. As a result, it became fashionable in seventeenth-century England to wear hats decorated with small mirrors.

Have you ever looked at yourself in a *three-way mirror* (a mirror with two other mirrors placed at angles to it)? You can see yourself reflected an infinite number of times in the mirrors. Looking in a three-way mirror gives you the feeling that there is another world beyond the surfaces of the mirrors. It was that illusion that inspired Lewis Carroll when he wrote *Through the Looking-Glass*, the sequel to *Alice's Adventures in Wonderland*. The story starts with Alice stepping through a mirror and into a magical kingdom.

In Through the Looking-Glass, *Alice climbs up on a mantel and passes through a mirror into a world of talking flowers, white rabbits, and a chess game where the pieces are alive.*

J. K. Rowling continued the tradition of magic mirrors in her book *Harry Potter and the Sorcerer's Stone.* One day, Harry comes upon a mirror in an empty room. When he looks into it, he sees his dead parents looking happy and alive. He can barely pull himself away from the sight. But, like all mirrors, even magic ones, it reflects the truth. This magic mirror reflects Harry's greatest desire: to have his parents come back to life.

Have you ever looked
at yourself in a *funhouse mirror*?
Mirrors can play all sorts of seemingly magical tricks because they can subtly distort reality.
Funhouse mirrors can make your reflection look long and
thin or short and fat. Because we are used to flat mirrors that
reflect the world accurately, we can be surprised, delighted, and
sometimes appalled at the images a wavy mirror produces.

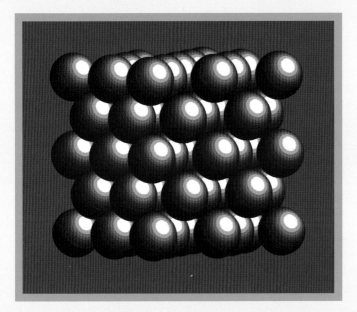

The molecules of most solids are arranged in a regular and orderly pattern.

The molecules in glass are arranged randomly.

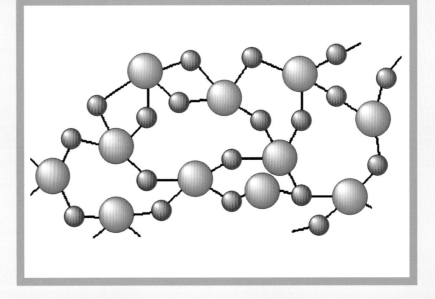

28

CHAPTER THREE

The Science of Glass

GLASS: LIQUID OR SOLID?

Glass is a most unusual substance. Scientists categorize matter (anything that occupies space and has mass) into three types: solids, liquids, and gases. So, what is glass? You might say, "a solid, of course," but the answer is not as simple as that.

If you could look at solids through an electron microscope that lets you see the substance's individual atoms, you would see that solids have a regular structure. Their atoms or their molecules (which are combinations of atoms) are arranged in a pattern, like bricks in a wall or cannon balls piled up in a pyramid. Solids are also rigid.

When solids are heated, their molecules absorb the heat energy and begin to vibrate. When they reach a specific melting point, the molecules move out of their regular structure and begin to move past one another in a disordered way. The solid has become a liquid. Ice is a familiar example: When an ice crystal reaches 32°F (0°C), it changes into water. Because solids have a regular molecular structure, they have a definite shape and volume.

The molecules of liquids have very little pattern or order. They are randomly arranged. A liquid is not rigid and has no definite shape, but it does have a definite volume. (Gases, in addition to having no molecular pattern or definite shape, have no definite volume. Molecules of gas can be pressed together into a smaller volume or allowed to expand to occupy more space.)

Glass is different from most solids because glass has no fixed melting point. As glass gets hotter and hotter, it gets softer and softer and more and more runny. There is no single temperature at which glass melts. In addition, as hot liquid glass cools into a hard object, its molecules remain in a disorderly state. The molecules do not arrange themselves in a pattern as those in solids do.

In the past, some people argued that even solid glass flows like a liquid, just too slowly to notice in a lifetime. However, scientists have discovered that even two-thousand-year-old Roman window glass hasn't flowed perceptibly. (Of course, we don't know what would happen to a glass window over the course of millions of years.) Perhaps it is best to define glass as a unique kind of matter, one whose molecules are arranged randomly like a liquid yet are locked in a rigid position like a solid.

When any material breaks, the bonds between its atoms or molecules are pulled apart. As anyone who has tried to cut glass will tell you, it is hard to make glass crack along a straight line. Glass, with its randomly arranged molecules, breaks in a random, jagged way.

TRANSFORMING GLASS: RAPID COOLING

Remember the mysterious exploding Prince Rupert's Drops? The drops were made by allowing molten glass to drip into cold water. Like most substances, when glass cools, it contracts (shrinks). When a drop of molten glass hits water, the drop's outer layer quickly cools and shrinks. But because glass doesn't conduct (carry) heat well, the interior glass stays much hotter—for a little while—than the cool outer skin. Then, as the inner glass cools, it also has a tendency to contract. But because it is attached to the already rigid outer skin, it can't. The inner glass pulls in, strongly and uniformly, on the outer layer of glass. This force compresses (makes smaller) the outer layer. Compressed glass is very strong. It is so strong that even a hammer blow on its outer layer can't break it.

The pull of the inner glass on the outer layer is called tension. As soon as Prince Rupert broke the tail of the drop of glass (or even made a scratch anywhere on its surface), the outer layer was no longer uniformly compressed. The inner glass was suddenly able to pull in the outer layer. The glass imploded (burst inward), turning itself into a mound of glass powder.

Modern *tempered glass* also uses compression—created by tension between the inner and outer layers of glass—for strength. Tempered glass is about four times stronger than ordinary glass. It is used in the back and side windows of cars, skylights, and safety goggles.

Tempered glass starts with a sheet of ordinary glass. The glass is reheated to about 1150°F (620°C). Next, nozzles blast high-pressure air over the surface of the hot glass. The blast

Tempered glass works well for a car's side and back windows, but it is not considered the best choice for windshields, at least in the United States. Small stones, kicked up by traffic, often strike windshields. If a stone penetrates the outer surface of a tempered glass windshield, the glass will crumble. Instead, windshields are made of *safety glass,* which is a sandwich of two sheets of glass with a layer of plastic between them. If the outside layer of safety glass is broken, the plastic holds the broken pieces together. The inside layer is more likely to remain whole. *Bulletproof glass* is made from many alternating layers of glass and plastic.

lasts just a few seconds and cools the surface quickly while leaving the core hot. A little later, when the inner glass cools and therefore shrinks, it pulls in on the outer surface. This puts the outer layer under tension and creates a strong, compressed outer surface.

As you might expect, during manufacture the surface of tempered glass is carefully inspected for bubbles, flaws, and scratches that would weaken it. Tempered glass can't be made and then cut to fit because cutting the surface would destroy the uniform compression. Rather, it has to be manufactured to the particular shape needed. When tempered glass does break, it breaks into small rounded pieces, much like Prince Rupert's Drops.

TRANSFORMING GLASS: CHANGING THE INGREDIENTS

Glass cannot be broken simply by compressing it, but it breaks easily under tension. Imagine a rubber rod. Imagine bending it (putting it under tension). It would bend easily because the material is elastic, meaning it stretches without breaking. Imagine bending a glass rod. It would hardly bend at all before it suddenly broke. Cool glass doesn't hold up well under tension.

Has anyone ever told you not to pour hot liquid into a drinking glass? Here's why: When the hot liquid touches the inside of the glass, it makes the inner surface expand. The hot, expanding inner surface tries to stretch the cooler outer surface along with it. Because cool glass is not very elastic, a break develops in the outer surface wherever there is a tiny flaw, and the glass cracks. Glass does not do well when it is placed under tension created by thermal shock (a rapid change in temperature).

In 1915, Corning Glass Works developed a new kind of glass, which it named Pyrex. Corning replaced most of the sodium carbonate, or soda, in ordinary glass with boric oxide. Glass made with boric oxide expands much less with heat than glass made with soda. Pyrex and other heatproof glass are used in measuring cups, baking dishes, laboratory containers, and the windows in oven doors.

Optical glass, which is used for microscopes, binoculars, prisms, and spectacles and other lenses, must be very pure. It requires silica that is free of impurities, including the usual traces of iron that make ordinary glass just the slightest bit green. Lead and barium oxides are also added to the optical glass mixture to make the glass bend light better.

It takes a very high temperature to melt the mixtures that are used to make optical glass. The furnace must reach over 3150°F (1930°C) instead of the 2100∞F (1150∞C) that melts ordinary glass. Optical glass must also be cooled very slowly over several days so that no uneven stresses develop within the glass that would interfere with light passing through it.

Glass made from silica and soda, but no lime, is called *water glass*. Water glass can be dissolved in water. Before refrigeration was common, the shells of eggs were coated in water glass so that the yolks and whites inside wouldn't dry out. Water glass is also used in the manufacture of detergents, cardboard and paper, textiles, paints, and adhesives as well as in the tanning, pottery, and wood-processing industries.

TRANSFORMING GLASS: STRETCHING

When you bite into a slice of cheese pizza and then pull the slice away, sometimes you will find (to your embarrassment) that a long thread of cheese connects your mouth and the pizza. When a glassmaker dips a rod into molten glass, he or she can pull out a long string of glass in just the same way. But unlike cheese threads, as glass threads cool, they solidify into permanent *glass fibers*.

Glassmakers have been making glass fibers for as long as they've been making glass. It wasn't until the nineteenth century, though, that anyone found a practical use for them. In the 1870s glassmakers discovered they could weave glass fibers together to make glittering, if fragile, clothing. The fibers, though, were short and ragged and difficult to work with.

About 1890 an English physics teacher named Charles Vernon Boys discovered a way to make very thin, very long glass strings. He built a tiny crossbow, fitted it with an arrow made from a needle, attached a piece of straw to the eye of the needle, and dipped the end of the straw in a pot of molten glass. Then he fired the needle from the crossbow. When the needle landed, it had pulled out a glass thread 90 feet (27 meters) long but only one ten-thousandth of an inch in diameter!

TRANSFORMING GLASS: CHANGING THE COLOR

Many liquids, including water, oil, and honey, are transparent (meaning light passes through them). That's because the molecules in liquids are not rigidly bonded to one another. They're disorganized and only weakly bonded to each other. In fact, there are small gaps between the molecules of liquids that allow light to pass through. That's one reason why most glass, which has the random molecular structure of a liquid, is transparent.

But not all liquids are transparent and not all glass is either. Milk is white because tiny particles of milk fat suspended in the milk prevent light from passing through. Opaque glass has particles suspended in it, too. White glass is opaque because ashes of bone were added to the molten glass.

Glass can be transparent but also colored. To understand why some glass has color, you need to understand a little about the nature of light.

Charles Vernon Boys was a bit of an odd duck. He made his living as a teacher, but was far more interested in experimenting than teaching. According to one of his students, the writer H. G. Wells, Boys "messed about with the blackboard, galloped through an hour of talk, and bolted back to the apparatus in his room." His special interest was building delicate, complex machinery.

Electromagnetic energy travels in waves. Visible light is electromagnetic energy whose wavelength (the distance between the peaks of the waves) is between 400 and 700 nanometers (billionths of a meter). Our eyes and brain have evolved to perceive energy with wavelengths in that range as light.

Within that range, we perceive differences among the wavelengths as the different colors of the rainbow: red, orange, yellow, green, blue, indigo, and violet. Red, for example, has a wavelength of about 700 nanometers. Sunlight, which appears colorless, includes all the wavelengths in the visible spectrum.

When glass is colorless, there are no obstacles to any of the different wavelengths of sunlight. But when glass appears green, there is something in the glass that prevents light with a wavelength of about 550 nanometers from passing through. Something in the glass absorbs the light of this wavelength. In some green glass that something is iron oxide.

People learned by experimentation which metal oxides absorb various wavelengths of energy and were able to manipulate the ingredients of glass to produce a great range of colors. They also learned to add both metal oxides and bone ash to the melt to create colored translucent glass, which allows some but not all light to pass through.

CHAPTER FOUR

The Art of Glass Containers

In early medieval Europe, the ancient Roman art of making beautiful glass vases, cups, and bottles languished. European glassmakers made glass objects primarily to suit a purpose, such as holding wine or beer, and they spent little effort in making these objects attractive. It was glassmakers in Persia, Egypt, and Syria who kept the tradition of making glass beautiful alive and produced lovely engraved, gilded (decorated with gold), and enameled objects. Until about A.D. 1000, these Middle Eastern treasures were sold largely to Middle Eastern customers. Western Europeans were generally too poor to buy luxury goods, and transportation was too perilous—mainly because of robbers— to risk shipping.

VENETIAN GLASS

About 1000, as peace and prosperity began to return to western Europe, the island state of Venice, which is today part of

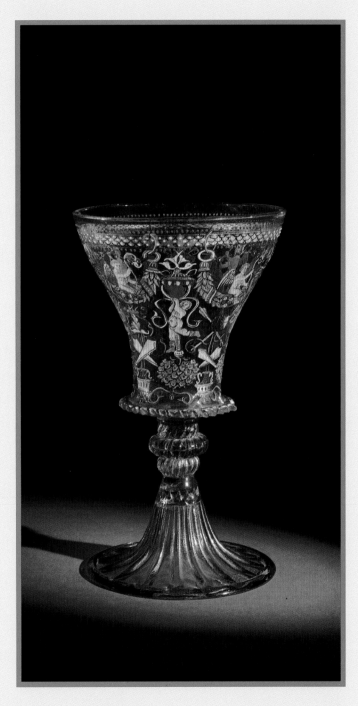

This colorful goblet decorated with gilding and enamel was made sometime between 1500 and 1525 by blowing glass into a mold.

Italy, rose to prominence and power. Venice built the world's most powerful navy, and when Venetian ships weren't involved in military actions, they were active in transporting goods between the "East," which meant the Middle East, India, and the Byzantine Empire (which included modern Greece, Turkey, Bulgaria, Serbia, and parts of Italy), and the "West," which meant western Europe. Venetian merchants bought grains, metals, and wool from the West and spices, dyes, silk, and glass from the East, and then arranged the sale of these goods in Venice.

Venetian merchants found it very profitable to sell eastern glass objects to western buyers. They realized it would be even more profitable if Venice produced its own glass for sale. Early in the thirteenth century, Venice conquered Constantinople (modern Istanbul, Turkey), the capital of the Byzantine Empire, where some of the world's most skilled glassmakers practiced their craft. The Venetians sent some of those glassmakers back to Venice, where they launched the Venetian glass industry.

Venetian glass of the thirteenth century was modeled on Middle Eastern glass and became popular in both the West and the East (where glassmaking was by this time in decline). As the Venetian glass industry boomed and became highly profitable, the government strictly regulated its operations. The hours of work and the kind of wood to be burned in the furnaces were specified in order to control the quantity and quality of the glass produced. Glassmakers were forbidden to travel out of Venice for fear that they would use their knowledge to start competing industries abroad.

In 1291 the government of Venice decreed that all the glass factories had to move to the nearby island of Murano. One reason for the decree was safety. Glassmaking factories housed hot furnaces that burned night and day . . . and frequently burned down, often setting fire to neighboring buildings. On Murano, fires wouldn't threaten homes and other businesses. The Venetian government also believed that by relegating glassmakers to the island, it could ensure that the secrets and profits of glassmaking stayed in the Venetian Republic.

A new era in glassmaking began at Murano in the mid-1400s when a glassmaker named Angelo Barovier invented *cristallo*, a thin, transparent, colorless glass made with sodium carbonate from certain vegetable ashes. Barovier's technique eliminated most of the bubbles and specks that marred earlier glass. Cristallo objects celebrated the beauty of the glass itself—its qualities and form rather than its color or the decoration painted or gilded on its surface.

Venetian glassmakers blew *cristallo into elegant forms like this wine glass from the mid-1500s.*

The inventiveness of the Murano glassblowers during the Renaissance period (roughly 1400 to 1700) is legendary. They perfected a style that is still popular today called *millefiori*, which means "a thousand flowers" in Italian. To make millefiori, the artist melted together long,

40

spaghetti-like pieces of brightly colored glass into a rod. Then he or she (there were several well-known female glass artists on Murano) cut the rod into thin slices, placed the slices side by side, and embedded them in clear glass. The result was what looked like a carpet of thousands of multicolored flowers. The millefiori could then also be blown into containers.

This millefiori bottle was made in Venice about 1500.

OPTICAL GLASS

The cristallo of Murano pleased the eye in more than one way. Sometime in the thirteenth century, glassmakers ground (shaped with an abrasive) and polished clear glass to form a magnifying lens. Optical glass was born.

The earliest people must have noticed that the domed shape of a raindrop makes whatever lies beneath it look larger. Ancient Greek and Roman writers knew that a glass globe filled with water would magnify items placed in or behind it. But it wasn't until the Middle Ages, sometime after

1100, that people put the magnifying ability of a clear, curved surface to work.

When the Crusaders returned to western Europe from their efforts to recapture Jerusalem in the 1100s, they brought back with them the writings of a gifted Arab mathematician named Alhazen. Among Alhazen's works were detailed studies of precisely how light is refracted (bent) by water and glass and how images are magnified. European monks read Alhazen's work with interest. As avid readers (and among the few literate people of the time), they recognized the practical value of his studies. They took pieces of rock crystal and the semiprecious stone beryl and ground and polished them into hemispheres. When they placed these hemispheres on top of writing, the writing was enlarged. The devices became known as *reading stones* because they helped those with poor eyesight read.

The glassmakers of Murano were familiar with reading stones. Rock crystal and beryl were expensive, so the glassmakers made them out of cristallo. But reading stones only magnified a few words at a time, were awkward to use, and couldn't help those who needed to write as well as read. Some other device was needed.

No one knows exactly who invented spectacles, but we do know they were invented in Italy in the last few decades of the thirteenth century. The earliest spectacles were made out of polished rock crystal, but the glassmakers of Murano soon were making them out of ground and polished cristallo. These first spectacles corrected for presbyopia, a form of farsightedness that many people over the age of forty develop that can be overcome with magnification.

This painting is one of forty frescoes painted by
Tommaso da Modena in 1352 that portray monks at work. These
are the earliest images we have of people wearing spectacles.

43

For several hundred years spectacles used only *convex* (dome-shaped) *lenses* that magnified objects and helped people see close objects better. In the 1500s spectacle makers invented spectacles with *concave* (inward-curving) *lenses*. Then people who had trouble seeing distant objects could also wear spectacles to correct their vision.

MICROSCOPES AND TELESCOPES

Microscopes have small lenses that greatly magnify objects. The earliest simple microscopes used drops of water or oil suspended in a tiny hole to magnify objects. The drop in the hole naturally had a rounded, convex shape that acted like a tiny but powerful magnifying lens.

In the middle 1600s, Antonie van Leeuwenhoek, an apprentice in a dry goods store in Holland, had to use a magnifying glass to count the threads in the cloth sold in the shop. (The greater the number of threads, the greater the value and price of the cloth.) Dissatisfied with the magnifying lenses of his day, this highly inventive young man learned how to grind and polish tiny, highly curved glass microscope lenses that were far stronger that any others of the time. About 1674 he used the lenses to discover bacteria, yeast plants, and blood corpuscles circulating in capillaries and revolutionized people's understanding of life on Earth.

About the same time in Holland, glass lenses also expanded people's understanding of life beyond the planet. Hans Lippershey, a Dutch spectacle maker, is credited with inventing the telescope about 1608. There is a story that Lippershey happened to look through two different-shaped spectacle lenses at once and was surprised to see that a distant church tower seemed to jump to the door of his shop. Lippershey's first idea was to use this phenomenon as a way to attract customers into his shop. He set up the lenses in his shop so people could see the magic (and then perhaps buy a pair of spectacles). Lippershey eventually enclosed the two lenses in a tube to make what he called a *kijkglas,* or "look glass." In 1608 he presented his invention to the government of Holland for use by the Dutch military.

Lippershey's invention was quickly copied (or may have been independently invented by others), and he never received a patent for it. News of the invention spread to Italy, where Galileo Galilei crafted his own version. It was Galileo who turned the telescope on the night sky and discovered that the moon has craters, that Jupiter has its own moons, and that

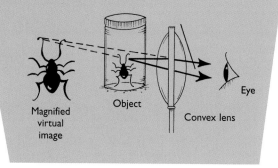

How do magnifying lenses work? When light passes through a glass lens, the light bends. Convex lenses have outwardly curving surfaces that bend light so objects seen through them appear larger. When you look through a convex lens, light rays that bounce off the object toward your eye are bent by the lens. Your eyes trace the rays of light back in a straight line and your brain "sees" a larger image.

Magnified virtual image

Object

Convex lens

Eye

Galileo's telescope was a *refracting telescope*. Refracting telescopes work by allowing light to pass through two lenses, one convex and the other concave. The problem with refracting telescopes is that all the colors of light that make up white light are bent at slightly different angles. The images seen through early refracting telescopes were fuzzy for that reason. Isaac Newton helped solve this problem by introducing curved mirrors to focus light in telescopes. Telescopes with mirrors are called *reflecting telescopes*.

the Sun has spots. Ultimately, the truth revealed by the telescope—that the Earth circles the Sun and not the other way around—changed the way people conceived of mankind's place in the universe.

GLASS ARTISTRY SPREADS

Venetian cristallo was clear and light, and glass artists could blow and coil it into fanciful shapes. Because cristallo was so delicate, however, it was a difficult glass to engrave. North of Italy, in Bohemia and Germany, glassmakers used somewhat different materials to make glass. They substituted potash (potassium carbonate) for soda and the resulting glass was harder, if not so clear or malleable (easy to form). With the new *potash glass*, Bohemian and German glassmakers were able to revive the ancient Roman tradition of engraving glass. By holding cold glass against a rapidly spinning engraving wheel, artists etched and sculpted detailed scenes on its surface.

In 1674 the art of glassmaking went in a new direction when Englishman George Ravenscroft patented a new glass. Ravenscroft incorporated lead oxide into his glass formula. His *lead-crystal* was heavy and crystal-clear, and drinking glasses made from it rang like a bell when tapped. In the mid-1700s,

Here a modern glassmaker uses a wheel-engraver to decorate glass.

This colorful bowl was engraved with a dragonfly motif in about 1900.

glass artists in England and Ireland developed techniques that took advantage of the ability of lead-crystal to refract and reflect light. They cut deeply into the surface of the glass, making geometric patterns that sparkled brightly in light.

At this time, candles were the source of much indoor light, but it took dozens of them to light a large room. In the mid-1700s, craftsmen began to decorate chandeliers (frames for candles hung from the ceiling) and candelabras (branched candlesticks) with pieces of lead-crystal. Each piece had been cut so that it had many facets (small, flat surfaces). When candlelight shone through the lead-crystal pieces, the light was refracted and reflected, which made the room brighter than it would have been with candles alone.

THE CRYSTAL PALACE

In 1851, England captured the imagination of the world with its magnificent Crystal Palace, built to house its Great Exhibition, a display of the best and most beautiful products of the Industrial Age. This was the first world's fair. The building, designed by British landscape designer and gardener Joseph Paxton, was constructed of glass panes supported by iron posts and beams. Paxton used familiar greenhouses as his inspiration.

The Crystal Palace was a marvel. It was huge: 1,848 feet (569 meters) long and 408 feet (126 meters) wide, or more than six football fields long and one football field wide. At its highest, it was about ten stories tall and it was built right over 90-foot (27-meter) trees! The building used 293,000 panes

The Crystal Palace

made of mouth-blown glass. In addition, there was a glass fountain nearly three stories tall at its center, which was made from 4 tons (3.6 metric tons) of glass.

Glass had long been used to cover windows in buildings, but until 1851 it had never before been used as a structural element in a building. The Crystal Palace made people look at glass in an entirely new way. It sparked inventors' and artists' imaginations. In the coming decades, they would develop dozens of new ways to manipulate glass.

Prince Albert, husband of Queen Victoria, conceived the notion of the Great Exhibition. He wanted to both celebrate the industrial and economic strength of Great Britain and its colonies and protectorates and to provide a model for the rest of the world. He wanted the building to be as magnificent and modern as the exhibitions inside—and it was. Unfortunately, the Crystal Palace is no longer standing. It burned to the ground in 1936.

CHAPTER FIVE

Modern Glass

FLAT GLASS

The glass panes of the Crystal Palace were made as glass panes had been for centuries: by blowing glass cylinders, cutting them lengthwise, and then flattening them. Making flat glass in this way was a slow process. The resulting panes were small, wavy, and flecked with tiny air bubbles. The view through them was always slightly distorted.

During the reign of France's King Louis XIV in the seventeenth century, French glassmakers discovered how to cast (pour) molten glass to make sheets of glass. The molten glass was poured from a pot onto a large metal plate and then rolled flat with a metal roller. This *plate glass* then had to be polished by hand. Although it was much freer of distortions and could be made in much larger pieces than cylinder glass, it was also extremely expensive. Only the very wealthy could afford plate glass.

By the beginning of the twentieth century, plate glass had come down in price. Electric grinders and polishers made production faster and cheaper. Then, in the 1930s, a new American

French mirror makers coated the backs of newly invented plate glass with silver to make these enormous mirrors at Louis XIV's palace at Versailles. Until this time, wavy glass caused even the best mirrors to distort reflections. The French mirrors were stunning for their clarity as well as their size.

process drew molten glass through two water-cooled rollers in a continuous ribbon of glass. The glass was finished simultaneously on both sides. Plate glass windows became common in storefronts and buildings around the world.

A revolution in window glass occurred in 1959 in England when Alastair Pilkington invented *float glass*. In the float glass process, molten glass flows continuously from a glass furnace onto the surface of a 2-inch- (5-centimeter) deep bath of molten tin. The molten glass floats on top of the tin and the two materials do not mix. The contact between the two materials produces a perfectly smooth, flat surface that does not need grinding or polishing. A stream of hot air blown over the upper surface polishes the other side of the glass. Today, about 95 percent of the world's flat glass is made with the float glass method.

Window glass not only lets light into a building, it keeps warm air inside in the winter and cool air inside during the summer. Today, *low-E* window glass turns float glass into a much more efficient barrier between inside and outside environments. Low-E glass is coated with tin or silver oxide. In the summer, the coating on the outside repels the sun's energy. In the winter, the coating on the inside reflects the building's heat back into the building. Yet while a low-E coating effi-

You have probably seen office buildings with colored windows. Sometimes the color results from added coatings that make the windows better insulators. The blue glass that you see in this Virginia building, for instance, may have copper in it. Other metals added to molten glass produce bronze, gold, and silver-colored glass.

ciently reflects heat, it allows 95 percent of the visible light to pass through. Sometimes, low-E windows are also *double-glazed*, which means that two sheets of glass are joined back-to-back with a tiny space enclosed between them. Argon gas, a good insulator, is sometimes injected between the two sheets to make the glass even more energy efficient.

GLASS BULBS

Since the ancient Egyptians first dipped a dung and clay core into molten glass to form a bottle, people have found glass to be an excellent material to contain liquids. More recently, glass has also been used to contain light. In the nineteenth century, clear glass tubes (called *chimneys*) helped to protect oil lamp flames from wind and the drafts that made them flicker or go out. But when Thomas Edison harnessed electricity to make light in 1879, glass became essential to lighting.

In the 1780s, Aimé Argand, a Swiss, invented the Argand lamp, the first lamp that used a glass chimney to protect the flame of a lamp. Air was supplied to the burning wick from below the chimney.

■ ■ ■

Incandescent (glowing) lightbulbs work because they contain a vacuum. Electricity heats the filament (the thread of metal inside) to a glow, but, without air, the filament doesn't burn. Why does a lightbulb burn out? Because its filament, made of tungsten, eventually fails when a critical number of atoms of tungsten evaporate from the filament's surface, making the filament so thin that it breaks.

If the vacuum in an incandescent lightbulb is filled with a gas, such as halogen, the bulb works longer. That's because the gas combines with tungsten deposited on the inside of the bulb and redeposits the tungsten on the filament. Bulbs filled with certain gases, such as neon or mercury vapor, don't use filaments. The gas itself glows when an electrical current is passed through it.

Using a ribbon machine, a worker produces lightbulbs.

Until 1922 lightbulbs were mouth-blown and very expensive (a bulb cost a worker about half a day's pay). Then Will Woods at the Corning Glass Works invented a machine that blew air through molten glass into a mold, where the bulb was formed. The machine could blow about 2,500 bulbs per hour. The cost of lightbulbs declined dramatically.

Today, the *ribbon machine* makes lightbulbs at the rate of 66,000 per hour. The machine moves a narrow ribbon of molten glass over a moving belt of steel that is perforated with holes. Bulb molds lie beneath the holes and puffs of air push glass against the mold, creating many bulbs at once.

GLASS FIBER

Inventors in the early twentieth century improved on Boys's needle-and-crossbow method (see Chapter Three) of making glass fibers. In 1932 a young researcher named Dale Kleist at Owens-Illinois glass company was trying to weld architectural glass blocks when a jet of compressed air accidentally hit a stream of molten glass. The air blew the molten glass into a spray of short, fine glass fibers. Later, Kleist used steam instead of compressed air and made even finer fibers. The engineers at Owens Corning (formed in the late 1930s by a merger of Owens-Illinois and Corning Glass Works) found that these glass fibers, known as *glass wool*, made excellent insulation that could be used inside the walls of buildings.

They also discovered that the glass wool could be used in textiles. Glass wool fabric could replace wool or synthetic fibers in draperies and other decorative fabrics. The fact that the fabric didn't wrinkle and wouldn't catch fire made it popular. The biggest problem was that the glass fabric couldn't be dyed with traditional dyes: Glass fibers wouldn't absorb anything. The fabric had to be coated or printed.

A kind of glass wool, called *fiberglass*, has somewhat longer fibers. Fiberglass was first made by forcing molten glass through tiny holes of a spinning nozzle. Centrifugal force pushed out longer glass fibers that were then collected on a conveyor belt. Owens Corning pioneered the use of fiberglass in boats. Fiberglass layered with plastic created a strong, moldable material that didn't need the sanding, caulking, and painting that took up so much of a wooden boat owner's time.

A kayaker paddles through lily pads in a fiberglass boat.

In 1947 the engineers at Owens Corning developed a technique for making a fiberglass chair. Designed by Charles Eames, the chair became a classic example of the marriage of design and practicality.

Today, fiberglass is the most popular material for pleasure boats. Some car bodies are made from fiberglass, too.

Other methods of making glass fibers evolved. One method involved suspending a glass rod vertically, heating its lower end, and drawing long fibers from it. Another was to shoot molten glass through pinprick holes in a dish. At first, the promise of glass fibers seemed to be in making fiberglass materials. But later in the twentieth century, the use of glass fibers revolutionized communications and computers.

Since the 1840s scientists had known that glass rods could transmit light. In 1841, Daniel Colladen, a Swiss scientist, sent light through covered streams of water, which acted like glass rods in their ability to convey light. In 1880 an American inventor named William Wheeler filed for a patent for glass "light pipes" that would carry light from a lamp in the basement to every room in the house, much like copper pipes carried water.

Light tends to travel in a straight line through a vacuum or through transparent substances. When the light hits another, less dense substance, the light bends. Light travels straight down a glass fiber until the fiber bends. Then the light hits the surface of the fiber (which is slightly less dense than the rest of the fiber), and bends at a small angle, as if the inner surface of the fiber was a mirror. The light continues to travel forward, bouncing off the inner walls of the glass fiber like water down a pipe. This phenomenon is called total internal reflection.

When long glass fibers were developed in the twentieth century, scientists found that light would travel down a glass fiber. Of course, one glass fiber transmitted hardly any light, so it made sense to bundle a large number of glass fibers together to send a greater amount of light. A German medical student named Heinrich Lamm bundled fibers together in 1930 and transmitted the first *fiber optic* image ever.

But Lamm and others discovered that when optical glass fibers were bundled together, not as much light came through as expected. Where the fibers touched, some light passed from fiber to fiber instead of reflecting inward. In addition, when the fibers touched each other, they made minute scratches. Those scratches also allowed light to leak out and made the fiber more likely to break.

In the 1950s scientists figured out how to coat glass fibers with plastic. The plastic cladding protected the surface of the glass and kept light from leaking out. Today, glass fiber is made and coated at the same time to keep the glass in its flawless condition.

The optical glass fibers in use today are made by fusing ultra pure vapors of silica and other chemical ingredients in a tube, applying great heat, and then allowing gravity to draw out an ultrathin fiber from the molten glass. Today's optical glass fibers are so thin they are no wider than a human hair and can be formed into a loop with a diameter of only one-eighth of an inch (30 millimeters). Modern optical glass fiber-making processes produce a fiber that is virtually flawless, without the tiny cracks that might allow the fiber to break apart under tension.

At the start of the twenty-first century, optical glass fibers carry most of our long distance telephone calls. To send a message, a laser (which produces a high-energy light beam) at one end flashes on and off, producing the bits of information that are detected at the other end. Because the laser can turn on and off several billion times per second and because light travels fast, one pair of glass fibers can carry hundreds of thousands of two-way conversations. Compare that to the twenty-four conversations that copper wires can carry!

The glass in glass fiber optics is so transparent that if someone used it to make a window several miles thick, it would be perfectly clear!

VITRIFICATION OF RADIOACTIVE MATERIALS

For nearly fifty years, the United States made plutonium-239, a highly radioactive material used in nuclear bombs. In making plutonium, a lot of dangerous radioactive waste was produced. Some of the "low-level" (not too dangerous) waste has been converted to a kind of cement and buried in vaults deep in the ground. Other, more hazardous, waste is too radioactive to dispose of in this way. The more hazardous waste, which looks like dark sludge, needs to be contained in a more durable material.

At a site outside Savannah, Georgia, a processing plant now turns the highly radioactive sludge into radioactive glass. In a process called *vitrification* (*vitrum* is Latin for "glass"), the sludge is mixed with the familiar ingredients of glass—silica, soda, and lime, as well as metallic oxides and boron—and heated for about sixty hours to over 2100°F (1150°C). The molten glass is then poured into thick steel canisters that hold 3,700 pounds (1,680 kilograms) of glass and contain the radioactivity. The canisters are sealed and buried in underground vaults.

Radioactive materials slowly decay (meaning they lose radioactivity), but the process can take tens of thousands of years. The objective in nuclear waste disposal is to prevent radioactive materials from getting into the environment before the decay is complete. That's why radioactive materials are bound into glass. Glass doesn't dissolve in water or interact with chemicals. (Laboratories use glass for flasks and other containers for this reason.) So even if the containers around the glass corrode, the likelihood is that the radioactivity will stay in the glass and not seep into the ground.

In the United States, vitrification is also being used to contain soil contaminated with dangerous chemicals such as arsenic, mercury, and dioxin. In Japan, the ashes of city wastes are vitrified. In France, each week a hundred tons of asbestos, an old insulating material whose delicate fibers can cause lung disease, are turned into a glassy substance. Inventors are considering isolating all kinds of dangerous materials by locking them up in glass.

NEW ART GLASS

The first glass ever made was formed into beads and other objects designed just to please the eye. Over the millennia, glass artists have continued to use glass to express their artistic ideas. While glassmakers made goblets, windows, chandeliers, and vases for a practical function, they also often reveled in the beauty of their material. They played with the form, color, and surface design of glass to turn useful objects into art.

In the 1960s the studio glass movement started at the University of Wisconsin under the guidance of Harvey Littleton. In the twentieth century, until the early 1960s, blown glass was produced only at expensive and complex furnaces. In 1962, Littleton, with the technical assistance of Dominic Labino, a chemist and inventor from Ohio, invented a relatively inexpensive small furnace capable of melting glass on a small scale. Artists were then able to melt glass in furnaces in home studios.

Studio glass artists make glass objects as pieces of art with little or no practical function. Glass has joined canvas and paint, wood, and clay as popular media for making works of art. The studio glass movement has been centered near Seattle, Washington, for many years. One of the most popular glass artists of the area is Dale Chihuly. Chihuly works in a glass studio in a converted factory he calls The Boathouse. The Boathouse is, in a sense, a re-creation of the experience of glassmakers on the island of Murano during the Renaissance. Chihuly and a large group of fellow glassmakers work together to create stunning works of art in glass.

In the 1980s, Chihuly worked on a series of wavy pieces that look like large glass anemones and seashells rippled by seawater. In the 1990s he turned his attention to making very large glass pieces designed to be installed in public places. From 1994 to 1996 he and his Boathouse colleagues produced fourteen huge glass chandeliers that were hung over the canals of Venice.

SURPRISING GLASS

Glass is the most surprising material. No other material can take so many forms and serve so many functions, from carrying phone conversations to containing radioactive materials to stunning the eye with exquisite form and glowing color.

Glass has lots of surprises left for us to discover. One promising area researchers are exploring is the possibility of making a fabric that is part glass and part plastic. Such a fabric would have the elasticity of plastic but it wouldn't burst into

Chihuly glass objects are often very large, and it takes many people to make them (above). Timing and coordination among the glassmakers is critical. (You don't want to bump into someone spinning a red-hot seashell of glass!) Chihuly himself no longer blows glass because he was blinded in one eye in a car accident. Because it takes two eyes to be able to judge the distance of objects, he now designs his works on paper and directs the glassmakers in his studio. Chihuly studied in the famous Venini Fabrica, a glass studio in Murano, Italy. It was here that he came across some elegant and ornate vases from the 1920s that inspired his Venice chandeliers. His chandeliers, like the one on page 65, are a marriage of vase and chandelier.

Glass can be found in many of the objects we use everyday—from our drinking glasses to our computer screens to the camera we use to make movies for the big screen.

flame when exposed to high heat. Like glass, it would just melt! It would be great for making fireproof carpets and upholstery fabrics. Other scientists are working on covering glass with very clear, strong plastic. Plastic-coated glass is already being used to make windows that can withstand the impact of a tree branch tossed by hurricane-force winds. It doesn't take a crystal ball to see that glass will continue to help (and delight) us in the twenty-first century!

Glass is also fun. In the 1920s and 1930s, a game with glass marbles called Ringer became very popular. Ringer is played in a 10-foot- (3-meter-) diameter dirt ring. Thirteen marbles (called ducks) are arranged in the middle of the ring. The object is to shoot the marbles out of the ring by flicking a marble "shooter" at them. The player who shoots the greatest number of ducks out of the ring wins. Glass marbles are still made today. One West Virginia company, Marble King, makes a million glass marbles per day. These beautiful marbles were made by another West Virginia company, Gibson Glass.

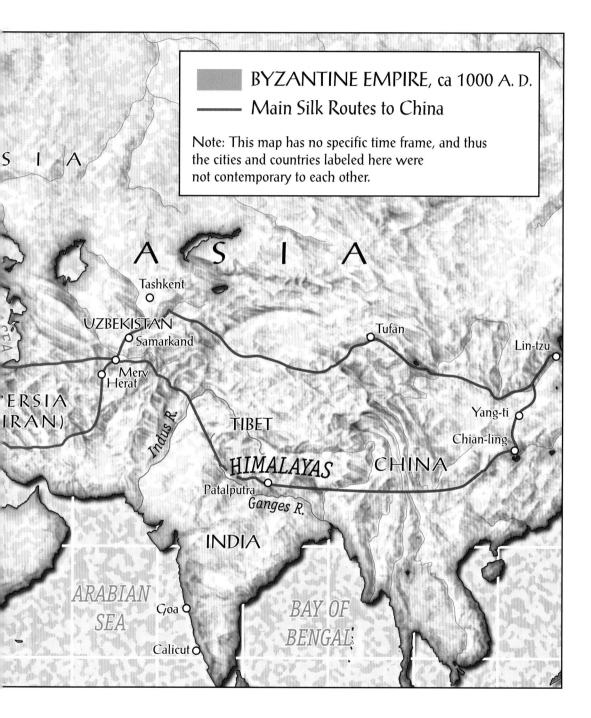

BYZANTINE EMPIRE, ca 1000 A. D.

Main Silk Routes to China

Note: This map has no specific time frame, and thus the cities and countries labeled here were not contemporary to each other.

ASIA

Tashkent

UZBEKISTAN
Samarkand

Tufan

Lin-tzu

Merv
Herat

PERSIA
(IRAN)

Yang-ti

TIBET

Chian-ling

HIMALAYAS

CHINA

Indus R.

Patalputra

Ganges R.

INDIA

ARABIAN SEA

Goa

BAY OF BENGAL

Calicut

Timeline

B.C. **2500** Mesopotamians begin making glass in the form of beads and small pieces of jewelry

1500 Egyptians begin making glass and pioneer core method of making bottles

A.D. **100** Romans make glassblowing an industry; glass containers become available to ordinary people

500s After the fall of the Roman Empire, European glassmaking declines

800s Glassmaking flourishes in the Middle East

1000 Stained glass production begins in northern Europe

1100s European crusaders bring back writings of Arab mathematician Al-hazen, which include studies of how water can be used to magnify images

1204 Venice conquers Constantinople and brings back some of the best of Byzantine glassmakers, launching great era in Venetian glassmaking

Late 1200s Italian glassmakers invent spectacles

1291 Venice moves its glassmaking industry to Murano

1300s	Tamerlane conquers much of the Middle East, ending the greatest era of Islamic glass
1400s	Beginning of the Renaissance in Europe
1450	Angelo Barovier invents cristallo
1608	Hans Lippershey invents telescope, which Galileo then refines
1680	French glassmakers invent new method for making plate glass
1640	Prince Rupert of Bavaria introduces exploding glass drops in England
1670s	Antonie van Leeuwenhoek observes microscopic life with his newly invented microscopes
1674	George Ravenscroft invents lead crystal
1784	Benjamin Franklin invents bifocals
1851	Crystal Palace built in England to house the Great Exhibition
1870s	First fiberglass cloth invented
1879	Thomas Edison creates first vacuum lightbulb
1880	William Wheeler files for "light pipes" patent
1893	Blenko Glass Company opens
1914	Corning Glass invents Pyrex
1922	Ribbon machine for making glass bulbs quickly invented
1930s	Heinrich Lamm transmits first fiber optic image
1959	Alastair Pilkington invents float glass
1960s	The studio glass movement begins

Glossary

annealing oven: an oven used to cool glass slowly

bifocals: spectacles that have two portions of glass and allow the wearer to focus on objects at two different distances

blowpipe: the hollow iron pipe that a glassmaker uses to blow molten glass

bulletproof glass: a multi-layered sandwich of glass and plastic

came: a strip of lead that holds stained glass pieces and a completed stained glass panel in place

cameo glass: layered glass of different colors that is sculpted to portray a person or a scene

chimney: a clear glass cylinder that protects a lamp or candle flame from wind or drafts

concave lens: inward curving lens

convex lens: outward curving lens

cristallo: a thin, transparent, colorless glass pioneered in Venice, Italy, and made with sodium carbonate from certain vegetable ashes

crown: a round piece of glass formed by spinning a hot glass bubble on the end of a pontil

cylinder glass method: a method of making flat glass by shaping a mouth-blown sphere into a cylinder, cutting it lengthwise, and flattening it

double-glazed glass: two sheets of glass back-to-back with a tiny space enclosed between them

enamel: a glass-based surface covering usually fused by heat to an object

fiberglass: a material made of extremely fine glass fibers

fiber optic: glass fiber used for transmitting images

float glass: glass that has been flattened by being poured onto the surface of a bath of molten tin

funhouse mirror: a mirror designed to distort reality

gather: a thick glob of molten glass

glass fibers: extremely fine threads of glass; can be woven into cloth

glass wool: short, fine glass fibers made by blowing compressed air or steam across a molten stream of glass and used for insulation

grisaille: a dark brown enamel paint

lead-crystal: glass that contains lead oxide and is especially refractive

low-E glass: glass that has been coated with a metal oxide to prevent heat from passing between the inside and outside of the glass. Low-E is an abbreviation for "low-emissivity"

luster painting: a coating of paint made of oil mixed with silver, copper, or gold that, when heated, bonds with a glass surface and turns it a glittering amber color

marver: to shape and smooth a glass object by rolling it on a steel table

melt: the heated, liquid mixture of silica, soda, lime, and other ingredients used to make glass

millefiori: decorative glass made by fusing brightly colored glass rods, cutting them crosswise, joining them in new groups, and embedding them in transparent glass

mold-blowing: forming glass objects by blowing glass into a mold

obsidian: a kind of glass formed in volcanoes

optical glass: high-quality, color-free, highly refractive glass used in lenses

plate glass: thick, high-quality window glass

pontil: a metal rod that is used to remove a hot blown-glass object from a blowpipe

potash glass: a hard glass containing potassium, developed to withstand engraving

Prince Rupert's Drops: strong glass created by allowing molten glass to drip into cold water

reading stone: a piece of rock crystal or beryllium that was used for magnification for reading

reflecting telescope: a telescope in which mirrors focus light

refracting telescope: a telescope that works by allowing light to pass through two lenses, one convex and the other concave

ribbon machine: an assembly-line machine for making lightbulbs from a narrow ribbon of molten glass

safety glass: a sandwich of two sheets of glass with a layer of plastic between them

tempered glass: glass that has been cooled in such a way as to create tension between the outer surface and the inside of the glass, thereby strengthening it

three-way mirror: a mirror with two other mirrors placed at angles to it

vitrification: the process of turning substances into glass

water glass: glass that is water-soluble because it is made without lime

wheel-engraver: a wheel used to engrave glass

witches' balls: balls of glass filled with water or herbs, thought by some to have magical powers

For More Information

BOOKS

Ellis, William. *Glass: From the First Mirror to Fiber Optics, The Story of the Substance that Changed the World*. New York: Avon Books, 1998.

Glass: 5,000 Years. Edited by Hugh Tait. New York: Harry N. Abrams, Inc., 1991.

Halliday, Sonia and Laura Lushington. *Stained Glass*. New York: Mitchell Beazley Publishers, 1976.

Zerwick, Chloe. *A Short History of Glass*. New York: Harry N. Abrams, Inc. in association with The Corning Glass Museum, 1990.

WEB SITES

Corning Glass Museum
www.cmog.org

Glasslinks
www.glasslinks.com

Glass on Web
www.glassonweb.com

Index

About the Author

Ruth G. Kassinger is a writer, teacher, and consultant. She has written books on the U.S. census and on the history and science of inventions. She also writes articles on science and technology for *The Washington Post* and *Science Weekly*. She lives outside Washington with her husband, three daughters, and a small white dog.